FROM MUSTANGS TO MOVIE STARS

From Mustangs to Movie Stars

FIVE TRUE HORSE LEGENDS OF OUR TIME

BY LAUREL VAN DER LINDE

The Millbrook Press, Brookfield, Connecticut

Cover photograph courtesy of Robert Maier/Animals, Animals

Photographs courtesy of Jim Hansen: p. 12; Dave McRitchie: pp. 15, 17, 20; Giraudon/Art Resource: p. 24; UPI/Bettmann: pp. 26, 33, 39; AP/Wide World Photos: p. 30; Fleishman Hillard Inc.: pp. 36, 41 (photo by Bill Stover); Alix Coleman: pp. 44, 45; Bob Langrish: pp. 49, 55; Tony Parkes: p. 56; Nancy Moran, Sygma: pp. 58, 63.

Library of Congress Cataloging-in-Publication Data
Van der Linde, Laurel, 1952–
From mustangs to movie stars: five true horse legends of our time
Laurel van der Linde.
p.   cm.
Includes bibliographical references (p.   ) and index.
Summary: Presents the stories of five great modern-day horses,
from the Thoroughbred Native Dancer to the movie horse Cass Olé.
ISBN 1-56294-456-8
1. Horses—Biography—Juvenile literature.   [1. Horses.]
I. Title.
SF302.V36   1995   636.1—dc20   94-25866   CIP   AC

Published by The Millbrook Press
2 Old New Milford Road, Brookfield, Connecticut 06804

For Avalon

Many thanks to the following:

The American Jockey Club for the
racing records of Native Dancer.

Fleishman Hillard for information
on the Budweiser Clydesdales.

Melodee Spevack, for introducing me to Boomerang, and
Fiona Dowley for her insight into this horse.

Kelly O'Leary and Ginger Scott for sharing
the lovable J. B. Andrew.

The International Arabian Horse Association
and the Arabian Horse Registry of America, Inc.,
for their assistance with Cass Olé.

Special thanks to Mrs. Gerald Donoghue, Corky Randall,
and Dr. Elena Villavincencio, who graciously and
unselfishly recalled their personal memories of the
beautiful black stallion and without whose help
the story of Cass Olé could not have been included.

CONTENTS

INTRODUCTION

WHAT IS IT ABOUT THE HORSE that captures the imagination? Certainly no other animal has a more romantic image. Standing on a hilltop, silhouetted against the sky, or running free with mane and tail streaming in the wind, the horse is a symbol of qualities people everywhere admire—strength, grace, beauty, power, independence.

Of course, horses have been much more than symbols. For centuries they were part of everyday life—the most common form of transportation for people in many parts of the world. Horses drew plows over farmers' fields, carried riders on journeys long and short, and pulled coaches, buggies, and the wagons that delivered milk and collected trash. They carried the mail, raced through city streets drawing fire engines, and brought the doctor when illness struck. Mounted soldiers—the cavalry—formed the elite brigades of armies.

How the horse entered into this partnership with people will forever remain a mystery. In the wild, the more alert a horse was to its surroundings, and the faster it could run, the better able it was to escape predators. Horses survived for thousands of years by being tough, fast, and savvy. And any horse is strong enough to overpower a person. Why, then, do horses submit to the wishes of human beings?

For whatever reason, long ago horses and people came to depend on each other. Today horses are no longer part of ordinary life. But the bond remains between horses and people in the show ring and in sport and pleasure riding. The relationship between horse and handler is special. Each becomes the other's companion, and they often understand each other in ways that need no words.

Over the years some horses, and some partnerships between horses and people, have gained special renown. Anyone who knows and loves horses has probably heard the tale of how Alexander the Great tamed Bucephalus. It's hard to picture Napoleon without his famous horse Merengo. And for every famous horse, there are dozens of stories of less well-known horses with exceptional courage and steadfastness.

Horses of our time are no less talented and have no less "heart" than those of the past. The true stories in this book make that point clear. The horses are of different breeds—Thoroughbred, draft horse, Arabian, even a wild mustang. They represent many different worlds, from the demanding sport of show jumping to the unique work of moviemaking. But each story is remarkable, making these horses true legends of our time.

J.B. Andrew

THE UGLY DUCKLING

The mustang has long been a symbol of the American West. Surviving for centuries on the plains and in the mountains, the herds of these wild horses have come to signify strength and independence. The pursuit, capture, and taming of the mustang have been an ongoing source of fascination as well as continuing conflict.

The mustang is a descendant of the horses brought from Spain five hundred years ago by Spanish explorers. On the backs of these animals, the Spanish *conquistadors* easily dominated the native peoples of the New World. The Spanish landholdings included Mexico and much of South America and spread north into what is now the southwestern part of the United States.

Over the years, horses wandered from the Spanish settlements. Left on their own, these horses banded together, becoming as wild as the vast American plains they now called home. Herds roamed farther west into what are now the states of Nevada and California and as far north as Oregon. These wild Spanish horses were given the Spanish name *mesteño*, which means "strayed." Over time, the Spanish name was Americanized into the word "mustang."

Wild horses roam free in central Nevada.

As time passed and the frontier of the United States was pushed farther and farther west, settlers established ranching operations for cattle and sheep. To the rancher, the mustang was a "magnificent nuisance."

In the wild, the mustang herds bred at will. The population of wild horses overflowed onto government grasslands, competing with the ranchers' livestock for food. Like the Spanish before them, the ranchers also lost horses to the wild herds. Domestic mares of all breeds, from stocky quarter horses to big plow horses, now ran with the wild herds. With the mixing of these different breeds, the blood of the mustang was no longer of pure Spanish origin. The name mustang now refers to any wild horse, whatever the blood.

The overpopulation of mustangs continued to plague ranchers. They took matters into their own hands, capturing some and slaughtering others. Shocked at the cruelty, the American public pressured the United States government to take control of the situation. In 1971 the federal government passed the Wild Free Roaming Horse and Burro Act, which made the mustang a national treasure. The care and protection of the wild horses were assigned to the Bureau of Land Management. Every year, this agency systematically rounds up mustangs and puts them into an adoption program.

J. B. Andrew's story starts like that of any mustang. He was born in the wilds of Nevada and roamed the Eugene Mountain range near Winnemucca for the first year of his life. Then, in November 1985, he was rounded up with others of his herd by the Bureau of Land Management and branded on the neck.

Under the government's "Adopt-a-Horse" program, some mustangs are shipped to the Colorado state prison in Canon City, to be used in the reform program there. The idea is to teach prisoners useful skills, so that they will be able to find jobs when they are released. One of these skills involves the handling and training of horses. When the mustangs arrive at the prison, the female prisoners teach the wild horses to accept a halter and to be led. The male prisoners put them under saddle. The horses are also named. The skinny black two-year-old was called Andy.

Meanwhile, Ginger Scott of nearby Golden, Colorado, heard of the "Adopt-a-Horse" program. She wanted to get a horse for her daughter and thought that adopting a mustang would be worthwhile, so she drove to the state prison to look over the herd.

Andy had been working under saddle only eight weeks when he met Ginger. Ginger looked into his dark gentle eyes and fell in love. She asked to see him work. "You don't want this horse," said the representative from the Bureau of Land Management. "His head is too big." But the gawky gelding had already won her heart.

The prisoner who had trained Andy rode him in a field. Ginger was impressed by Andy's freedom of movement. "He looked like a big rocking horse," she remembered. Ginger immediately made the arrangements to adopt Andy—for $125 and a pair of cowboy boots for the prisoner who trained him.

At first, Ginger concentrated on fattening up the ungainly 16-hand youngster. Her original idea was to use him as a western pleasure horse, so she took him to western trainer Mark Boyle for additional work. But Andy's large size and big stride made him unsuitable as a western mount. Boyle suggested the mustang might make a dressage horse.

As ballet is to dance, dressage (pronounced like massage) is to equestrian disciplines. The word is French, meaning simply "training."

J. B. Andrew's kind expression
won his new owner's heart.

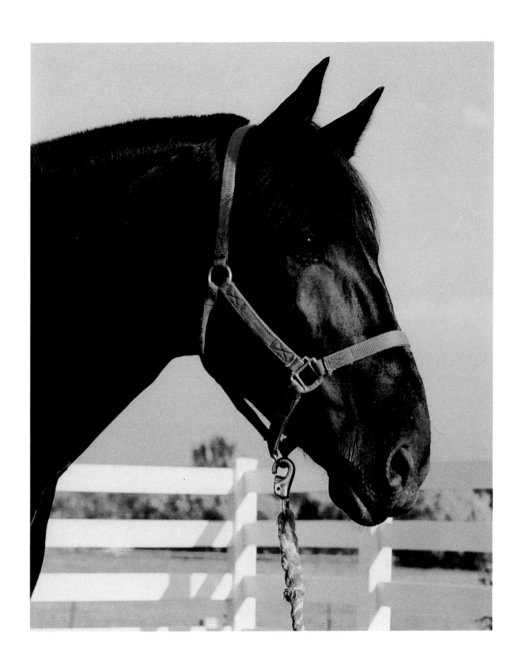

In dressage, the horse executes precision movements in response to subtle commands from the rider. But dressage is also a philosophy of working the horse by using kindness, patience, and understanding.

The training methods that are the foundation of dressage date from the ancient Greek cavalry. The horse is not asked to perform anything it cannot do naturally. Using slow and methodical techniques, the trainer works to develop a spirit of cooperation, so that horse and rider become a team.

Dressage is a structured way of training. For the horse it is very much like going to school. There is a specific amount of work that the horse must accomplish. In the same way that a child's education is developed over twelve grades, the education of the horse is structured into ten levels. Before a horse can move up from one level to the next, he must pass a series of three or four tests within each level. Of course, as the horse graduates each stage of training, more demanding movements are required of him.

The horses seen in today's dressage competitions are big, 16 hands or more. They have large strides to accomplish the demanding movements required of them. In size, Andy fit the profile of a dressage horse. What didn't match was his breed. Dressage horses are usually carefully bred warmbloods from Germany, Holland, or the Scandinavian countries. For a wild animal of unknown breeding to compete in the dressage arena against expensive European imports was unheard of—until Andy.

Following Boyle's advice, Andy was taken to Table Mountain Ranch for dressage training. It was here he met Kelly O'Leary. As Kelly's

Skinny and awkward when he came from the range, Andy filled out with good care and training.

horse recently had been injured, her instructor suggested to Ginger that perhaps Kelly and Andy could work together. Ginger agreed to the experiment.

Andy was still an "ugly duckling" when Kelly met him in the spring of 1989. "He had these big platter feet, no back end, was skinny and had a huge head," she recalled. Having grown another 3 inches (8 centimeters), he was awkward. It was no surprise that when Kelly first rode Andy he was unbalanced in his movements. When she asked him to canter, he kicked at her legs. Still, there was something lovable about the scrawny, oversized horse, and Kelly continued to ride him.

Kelly found Andy to be "a regular kind of guy," not only intelligent but cooperative. Andy tried hard in his work sessions. If he didn't understand something, he would shake his head back and forth in the bridle. It was his way of asking Kelly to explain exactly what it was she wanted him to do.

The two became a team. As their wild herd instinct remains strong, mustangs often see their trainer as the herd leader and bond with him or her. Andy could readily identify Kelly's moods. On days when she came to the barn "out of sorts," he would simply walk away from her and stand at the other end of the pasture.

After a year of working together, Kelly wanted to get another opinion as to how she and the horse were doing together. She decided to take Andy to a clinic conducted by German dressage trainer Jan Ebeling. As Ebeling had never seen the pair work before, Kelly thought that she would get an accurate evaluation. Ebeling was impressed. At first he assumed that the horse was some kind of warmblood, and he was surprised to learn that Andy was actually a wild horse.

The time had come for Andy to take the next step—into the show ring. As it happened, a show recognized by the United States Dressage Federation (USDF) was scheduled at the barn where Andy was pastured.

In his first year of working with Kelly, Andy had mastered the movements required at Training Level, the earliest stage of dressage training. His work at First Level was progressing well, so it was decided that for his first show Andy would perform First Level tests. He would be competing against dressage horses of various breeds.

Dressage horses are usually given elegant names, and Ginger felt that Andy's name needed some improvement. But she didn't want his new name to overshadow what he was. Since Andy is a nickname for Andrew, Ginger decided to change his name to J. B. Andrew. The J. B. stands for "jail bird."

Andy cooperated with the grooming procedures required before a horse can enter the show ring. First, he was given a bath. Then his feet were polished with black hoof polish. He stood still for what seemed an endless amount of time while Kelly braided his thick black mane into one-inch dressage braids.

Finally, it was time for J. B. Andrew to perform in the ring. In dressage only one horse performs at a time. Both horse and rider must concentrate. A hush falls over the crowd as each pair prepares to enter the arena. All that can be heard is the rhythmic fall of hoofbeats as the judges study and grade every move of the test. When the judges' scores were in, J. B. Andrew had placed fourth in First Level.

With such a good start, trainer and owner agreed that Andy should have a career as a dressage horse. Now his training began in earnest. To build his muscles, Kelly took him swimming in the nearby High Line Canal. Andy quickly mastered the other movements required to complete First Level.

Spectators and judges alike were intrigued by the big horse of undetermined breeding who continually beat the elite equines of pedigree. At one show, when Andy had taken a first, one of the competitors complained to the judge. "My horse should have won," she said. "This horse has no background." "But," said the judge, "he was the best."

In a dressage competition, Andy shows off the
balanced, floating trot that judges like to see.

As word of Andy's success spread, he earned an excellent reputation not only for himself but for the mustang. As a result he was invited in 1990 to perform at the Colorado Horse Fair. Kelly and Andy did a freestyle exhibition, or *kur*, in which horse and rider perform to music.

Andy was a hit. After he had completed his performances, the Bureau of Land Management booth was flooded with people asking for information as to how they could adopt a mustang. By the end of that year, the United States Dressage Federation ranked Andy thirty-seventh in the nation at First Level. He had also won the regional American Horse Shows Association (AHSA) dressage championship.

By the time another year had passed, Andy's body had filled out, finally balancing his large head. He and Kelly began coaching with Swedish trainer Claus Nielsen, showing at Second Level while learning Third Level movements at home. Andy took it all in stride. Showing had become such a common occurrence that Kelly now had to ride him energetically in the warm-up ring to make sure that he was alert and ready when his time came to perform.

During his third year of showing, Andy earned enough points to compete for the United States Dressage Federation championship in his region. Andy performed Second Level tests, competing against the best horses in five states. He missed the championship by only a few points and was awarded the reserve championship. He was now ranked twentieth in the nation.

Kelly and Ginger were thrilled. Andy, usually so calm and steady, was just as excited. The winners lined up behind the Regional Champion for their victory pass. The crowd cheered to see a home-grown American horse do so well. As the horses and riders began their tour around the arena, coach Claus Nielsen stood in the stands and shouted his approval as Andy passed by. This got Andy even more excited, and he shot ahead of the champion. It wasn't good equine etiquette—but it's not every day that a wild horse wins a USDF regional title.

From the wild Nevada range to the disciplined dressage arena, J. B. Andrew's story seems like a modern fairy tale. His intelligence and sensitivity made him easy to train. A true "people horse," Andy developed a large following at shows, and Kelly and Ginger had to scramble to prevent fans from feeding him the doughnuts and soda pop he loved.

The ugly duckling had indeed become a swan.

Native Dancer

THE GRAY GHOST OF SAGAMORE

On a cold day in the middle of December 1949, the gray Thoroughbred mare Geisha stepped off a van at the Daniel Scott Farm in Lexington, Kentucky. She had come from Sagamore Farm in Maryland to await the arrival of her foal.

The baby was due on the last day of February. But Geisha's foal did not arrive on time. He waited a full month past his due date to make his appearance shortly after 2 A.M. on March 27, 1950.

He would never be late again.

The colt came from a long line of Thoroughbred racing horses. His dam came from a line of sprinters. His father, Polynesian, had also made a name for himself as a short-distance runner. In keeping with the theme of his stallion's name, the mischievous youngster was named Native Dancer. In a short time, he would outstrip his sire's accomplishments.

Like all Thoroughbreds, Native Dancer was bred to run. The breed originated in England, where at the end of the fifteenth century stud farms were established by the British royalty to produce "running horses." Spanish and Italian horses were imported and crossed on such breeds as the Irish Hobby and Scottish Galloway. A century later, the blood of three Arabian stallions was added to the mix to both refine the English racing horse and increase its speed.

A racing scene painted in 1821 shows English Thoroughbreds streaking over a grass course. The breed was developed in England and brought to America.

The first of these was the Byerly Turk, captured by Robert Byerly at the Battle of Buda in 1690. The Darley Arabian was brought to England in 1704, and, finally, the Godolphin Arabian came to Britain in 1728. These three stallions were crossed on English horses to produce the Thoroughbred, the fastest breed of horse in the world.

As the breed's reputation for speed grew, Thoroughbreds were exported to other countries where racing was popular. This included the British colonies that later became the United States. Before long, stud farms were established in the new land to breed running horses. The United States has produced some of the world's greatest racing legends, among them Native Dancer.

In the fall of his first year, Native Dancer was shipped to California along with other yearlings owned by breeder Alfred Gwynne Vanderbilt. There, under trainer William Colin Winfrey, the rough-and-tumble gray colt was to be groomed for the racetrack. He was scheduled to run his first race at Santa Anita at the opening of the 1952 racing season.

Only one month into his training, on Christmas Eve morning, Native Dancer ran a quarter mile at the lightning speed of 23 seconds. He was promptly returned to Sagamore Farms on the East Coast. It was obvious to Vanderbilt that this colt had the talent needed to win the big races held in the East.

Native Dancer's reputation for speed preceded him before he ever ran a race. By the time he made his first start at the Jamaica track, outside New York City, on April 19, 1952, he was already considered the favorite to win the race. He did not disappoint those who had placed bets on him. With jockey Eric Guerin perched on his back, Native Dancer held back in the early part of the race, then swept past his competition to win by 4½ lengths.

Four days later, Native Dancer ran his second race. Again, he was the odds-on favorite. Again he won. His third start was just as successful, but an injury from that race kept him out of racing for three months.

The Dancer returned to the track in August and began making up for lost time. His first race back was the Saratoga Flash Stakes in Florida. He easily won by 2¼ lengths. One week later, he won the Grand Union Hotel Stakes. He finished up the month by winning the Hopeful, his fourth race in four weeks.

In his three-year racing career, the Thoroughbred Native Dancer won twenty-one races and lost only one.

Could anyone question that this was a horse born not only to run but to win? Yet there were those who doubted the Dancer. They pointed to his pedigree and insisted that he came from a line of short-distance runners or sprinters. They did not believe that Native Dancer could last at distances of a mile (1,600 meters) or more.

To end the debate, Vanderbilt entered Native Dancer in the East View Stakes. The race was 1¹⁄₁₆ miles (1,700 meters) long. It would be the ninth and last race of his first racing season. The big gray overtook every horse on the field, winning by 1½ lengths. He had proved that he not only could run fast but also last over long distances.

At the end of his first year on the track, Native Dancer was named Horse of the Year. He had won all nine races, regardless of length, and had earned $230,495 for his owner, a record for a two-year-old.

On a cold, wet April day in the following year, Native Dancer returned to the Jamaica track. The well-muscled gray now stood 16 hands high. When the starting gate sprang open and the horses charged onto the field, Native Dancer did not rush. He preferred to stay back, maintaining a steady pace. Then, when he was ready, he took over the track.

The big gray stood out among the more commonly colored bay horses on the track. Ghostlike, he moved up on the horses ahead of him and floated between them, overtaking them stride after powerful stride. It was this "come from behind" pattern that brought his fans screaming to their feet and earned him his nickname, the Gray Ghost of Sagamore.

Native Dancer's fame now extended beyond the stands, reaching people who had never been to the racetracks to see him run. In the early 1950s a new invention, television, began showing Thoroughbred racing, sending its black-and-white signal into the living rooms of millions of Americans. The excitement that Native Dancer provided on a Saturday afternoon made him one of the biggest TV stars of his time. An entire nation watched with anticipation as Native Dancer went to the post to run America's greatest race, the Kentucky Derby.

To the strains of "My Old Kentucky Home," eleven three-year-olds paraded to the starting gate at Churchill Downs in Louisville, Kentucky, on May 2, 1953. Storming out of the gate and cutting across the track to an early lead was Dark Star. As was to be expected, Native Dancer stayed back. But this time he got into trouble.

In horse racing, fractions of seconds are critical to winning a race. Coming around a turn, the Dancer was bumped by Money Broker. The jolt broke the rhythm and balance of the Dancer's stride. It cost him precious time.

Native Dancer's jockey, Eric Guerin, urged him forward, moving him up from eighth to fourth. To get out of a clump of horses on the rail, Guerin next moved the colt to the outside of the track. Now Native Dancer shifted into high gear. Using his record 29-foot (9-meter) stride, he began gaining ground on Dark Star. Neck to neck they ran and crossed the finish line—with Native Dancer less than a head behind Dark Star.

Understandably, owner Alfred Gwynne Vanderbilt was disappointed that Native Dancer had lost so important a race. Still, he congratulated Dark Star's owner, Harry Guggenheim, shaking his hand and saying, "If it had to be anyone, Harry, I'm glad it was you."

Native Dancer dealt with the defeat like the professional he had become. Two weeks later, while Dark Star rested, Native Dancer won the mile-long Withers Stakes at Belmont Park on Long Island, New York, by four lengths. One week after that, he again faced Dark Star for the second race of the Triple Crown, the Preakness Stakes, in Baltimore, Maryland.

In a repeat of the Kentucky Derby, Dark Star was the first out of the gate. But this time, Native Dancer was never far behind him. As Native

Dancer continued to move up on Dark Star, the Derby winner faltered and fell back. Native Dancer strode on to victory.

The Dancer now returned to Belmont for the Belmont Stakes, the third race of the Triple Crown. His only real opposition was Jamie K, a horse that had also run in the Preakness and that many people felt might win at the longer Belmont distance of a mile and a half (2,400 meters). There were those who still questioned whether Native Dancer could last over that long a stretch, but the colt silenced his detractors, coming in a neck ahead of Jamie K.

With win after win the Dancer was turning the three-year-old division upside down. Wherever he went, he drew a crowd. The excitement he caused affected not only his fans but seasoned track employees as well. One morning in August, he went for a gallop around the Saratoga track, in upstate New York. The track workers were so impressed by the colt's workout that they put down their brooms and applauded.

Native Dancer did not let the attention affect him. He also seemed to ignore weight. To keep a race competitive and fair, horses are required to carry a certain amount of weight. How much depends on their age, how many times they have raced, and how recently they have won. Throughout his career, the Gray Ghost was given more and more weight. And though he may have come out of the gate a little more slowly under more weight, it didn't stop him from winning.

"He hadn't a nerve in his body," said his trainer, William Winfrey. "(He was) the coolest, calmest horse before a race you ever saw." All he asked of his jockey was to stay on and not interfere. The Dancer would run his race his way. Jockey Eddie Arcaro found this out at the American Derby in 1953.

One week before the derby, Native Dancer's usual jockey, Eric Guerin, had been suspended for fouling another horse in the Saratoga

Native Dancer edges past Jamie K to win the Belmont Stakes.

Special. Native Dancer was left without a rider for the American Derby in Chicago. When Eddie Arcaro's mount Jamie K was pulled from the race, Winfrey asked Arcaro if he would like to ride the Dancer. Arcaro jumped at the chance to ride the horse he had not been able to beat for two years. He didn't know he had signed on for the ride of his life.

Carrying 128 pounds (58 kilograms), the Dancer began his race slowly. He had been having trouble with his left front foot and was in no hurry. Arcaro asked him to move up. Native Dancer obliged by passing a few horses, then eased up again, holding at fourth place. Arcaro was worried. Was this the horse he had been unable to beat?

Then he felt it. Native Dancer shifted gears. Arcaro was astounded by the surge of power from the animal under him. "He simply took off on his three sound legs . . . tore past the entire field and won pulling up. It was one of the bravest performances I ever knew. That Dancer—he was all heart and then some," the rider recalled.

Native Dancer came up lame on his left front foot after that race. Over the next few weeks five bruises were discovered on the hoof, and he was retired for the rest of the season. While he rested that winter, plans were being made for the 1954 season, including one race in England and one in France.

Native Dancer drew a large crowd to Belmont Park on May 7. The strapping four-year-old had "grown from boy to man." A new girth had to be found, as the old one was now too small. The win at Belmont was straightforward and confident—very different from the race he would run the following week.

For the Metropolitan Handicap, Native Dancer was asked to carry a burdensome 130 pounds (59 kilograms) of weight. Still, he was the odds-on favorite. Starting slowly, the Gray Ghost had passed just one horse after the first quarter of the race. With half the race run, he had put only two horses behind him. His fans were horrified. He was 8 lengths behind! Surely he couldn't catch up now.

But Native Dancer seemed to delight in the dramatic. Accelerating, he powered past the other horses, lining himself up with the leader, Straight Face. Only yards away from the finish line, he strode alongside the leader and crossed the line to win by a neck.

Native Dancer, however, had now bruised his right front foot. He was scratched from the races he was scheduled to run that spring and summer. By August, he was ready to run. When he arrived at Saratoga, his early-morning workouts drew crowds.

The Gray Ghost looked so good in his workouts that few dared to race against him. Only four horses challenged him for his next race. Weighted with 137 pounds (62 kilograms), the Dancer turned the race into child's play, winning by 9 lengths. It was his twenty-first win in twenty-two starts, a record that had never been achieved before.

Toward the end of August, the powerful colt came up lame on the right front foot again. The bruising had gone deep into the hoof. Native Dancer would never run again.

In October 1954, Native Dancer was given a retirement ceremony at the opening of the Woodward Stakes. Wearing special shoes to protect the injured hoof, the four-year-old looked ready to outrun any horse scheduled to race that day. The crowd gave him a standing ovation as his groom led him off the track for the last time.

The legendary Gray Ghost was again named Horse of the Year and returned home to Sagamore Farm where he stood at stud. There, he sired 306 foals, three of them champions.

Retired to stud at Sagamore Farm as a four-year-old, Dancer still had plenty of spark. Here he acts up as a groom struggles to control him.

Native Dancer not only left his mark on racing history but became a racing legend. He consistently conquered all track conditions, both good and bad. He beat the odds of distance and ran with more weight than any horse today would ever consider carrying.

The Gray Ghost of Sagamore died on November 17, 1967. He is buried at Sagamore Farm.

The Clydesdales

THE GENTLE GIANTS

They cause excitement wherever they go. Their massive bodies work together in perfect coordination as they step smartly, pulling a historic red wagon down the parade routes of America. The Clydesdales are a living reminder of the past, when people needed the draft horse to pull heavy loads.

The word "draft" (or "draught") comes from the Old English word for "pulling." With the invention of the wheeled plow in the sixth century, horses were used for farm work. As the work became more demanding, bigger animals were needed. Farmers bred their biggest mares to the biggest stallion they could find. Then they fed the offspring well to produce a workhorse of size and stamina.

In medieval times the region that is present-day Belgium, Holland, and northeastern France was known as the country of Flanders. This region, with its plentiful, rich pasture, was particularly successful at producing large horses. They were used not only as farm animals but also as war-horses. The medieval Great Horse, ancestor of the modern draft horse, was the only horse big enough to carry knights in heavy armor.

*This flashy Clydesdale team and their bright red
wagon turn heads wherever they go.*

The Flemish Great Horse was much in demand in Flanders and in other countries. Regular shipments were made to Scotland, particularly to the fertile valley or "dale" along the river Clyde in Lanarkshire. Early in the 1700s, one of the Dukes of Hamilton purchased six black Flemish stallions and brought them to this area. He made these horses available for breeding. At first the offspring were known as "the Clydesman's horses." Later, they were simply called Clydesdales.

When Scottish farmers immigrated into Canada, they brought their Clydesdale horses with them. In the mid-1800s, about the time of the American Civil War, these farmers began moving south. Their much-needed workhorses went with them, and the Clydesdale breed reached the United States.

The breed's hauling ability and gentle disposition made it the choice not only of farmers but also of brewery owners. Brewers needed massive amounts of horsepower to haul their heavy delivery wagons. While the quality of the brew was important, the success of a brewery might depend on how far its horses could pull a load in one day.

The Anheuser-Busch family has been involved with both the brewery business and horses for over a century. Adolphus Busch, who came to the United States from Germany in 1857, settled in St. Louis, Missouri, and married Lily Anheuser. Soon after, he was asked by his father-in-law to take over the operation of a brewery on Pestalozzi Street. Busch turned the small business into one of the most successful breweries in the country.

Busch knew his business depended on the draft horses that pulled his delivery wagons. For this reason, he made sure that the Anheuser-Busch animals received the best of care. He knew that a well-fed, well-treated animal did better work and more of it. Later, in 1885, when Busch built his own stable, he spared no expense. When the building was opened on the grounds of the Pestalozzi Street brewery, it was called an equine palace.

Busch passed on both the brewery business and his love of horses to his son, August A. Busch. When the younger Busch took over the management of the company in 1913, he sponsored contests on Sundays in which the wagon drivers paraded their teams for inspection. The team that was the best groomed, with "spit and polish" harness, won. His frequent companion at these Sunday turnout contests was his son, August A. Busch, Jr.

Of all the horses used in his father's brewery business, August, Jr., liked the Clydesdales the best. Often he would accompany the drivers on their delivery routes. Whenever he could, he tried to ride a wagon pulled by Clydesdales. Occasionally he was allowed to hold the reins. It is no surprise, then, that in later years he turned the Clydesdales into the symbol of the brewery.

At the beginning of the twentieth century, the brewery business was affected by two things: the invention of the motor car and Prohibition. Since 1900, trucks had begun to replace horse-drawn rigs. By 1917, Anheuser-Busch had its own fleet of delivery trucks. Two years later, Prohibition made alcoholic beverages illegal to produce.

Anheuser-Busch survived the next fourteen years by selling yeast, corn, and malt syrups. When it was announced that the law would be repealed, breweries began gearing up for production. New delivery trucks would again be needed. But as he made arrangements for the purchase of the trucks, August Busch, Jr., felt a sense of loss. He recalled the days he had spent as a child, riding alongside a driver behind a team of Clydesdales. No truck could ever replace the magnificent horses and wagons of his youth.

Intending to surprise his father, August, Jr., bought eight Clydesdales and harness in Chicago. The animals and tack were kept secretly at the brewery stables.

Minutes after midnight on April 7, 1933, the first beer in fourteen years came out of the Anheuser-Busch brewery. Later that afternoon,

*Draft horses were once widely used to pull heavy
delivery wagons. In this picture, a team leaves the
yard of a London brewery to make its rounds.*

August, Jr., walked into his father's office and asked him if he would like to have a look at the new car he had just bought. August, Sr., followed his son down to the street. Responding to a prearranged signal, a six-horse Clydesdale team pulling a red beer wagon appeared. From that day forward, the Clydesdales were a symbol for Anheuser-Busch.

Realizing how much excitement the hitch had caused, August, Jr., had the team shipped by train to New York City. There it presented two cases of beer to the man who had been a driving force in the repeal of Prohibition: Al Smith, former governor of New York. They then traveled to Washington, D.C., and delivered a case of beer to President Franklin D. Roosevelt at the White House. The Anheuser-Busch hitches have been on the road ever since.

The requirements for a hitch horse are very specific. The horse must be a gelding standing 18 hands high and weighing in at about 1 ton. He must be bay in color, with four white feet, a white blaze, and a black mane and tail. Since the Anheuser-Busch Clydesdales make about three hundred personal appearances a year, the hitch horses must have good dispositions.

Clydesdales are bred all over the world, not only in Scotland but in places as far away and exotic as New Zealand and Africa. The Anheuser-Busch Clydesdales are bred at two farms: on the West Coast in Romoland, California, and in St. Louis, Missouri, on Grant's Farm. Before the Civil War the farm was the home of Union General Ulysses S. Grant. Now its rolling acres support breeding stock imported from Scotland to continue the Clydesdale tradition in the United States.

When a foal is born in the spring at Grant's Farm, it spends the first six months at its mother's side. After it is weaned, a foal enjoys the company of the other foals of that year's crop, frisking in the pastures and growing. During this first year, the youngsters are taught to wear a halter and to be led.

A Clydesdale mare and her foal enjoy a pasture run.

By the time a colt is a yearling, he weighs about 1,100 pounds (500 kilograms). During his second year the youngster is taught to wear harness. After the tack has been fitted correctly, he is turned out in a paddock and allowed to run around so that he becomes accustomed to the equipment. A typical two-year-old Clydesdale weighs between 1,500 and 1,600 pounds (680 and 725 kilograms) and stands between 16 and 17 hands high.

As he begins his third year, he is taught to pull. Harnessed next to an older, experienced horse, the three-year-old is asked to pull a stone "boat." The trainer and an assistant stand on this slab, holding the reins of the harness. This easy weight teaches the young horse to lean forward into his collar.

He must also be fitted in iron shoes. As white feet are weaker than dark feet, great care is taken to protect the Clydesdale's hooves from injury. The shoe for a full-grown Clydesdale is twice the size and four times the weight of that worn by a saddle horse. A shoe for a Clydesdale measures more than 20 inches (50 centimeters) from end to end and weighs about 5 pounds (2.3 kilograms). A Clydesdale needs new shoes every five weeks.

A full-grown Clydesdale eats a lot of food. His two daily feedings will total 50 to 60 pounds (23 to 27 kilograms) of hay, 25 to 30 quarts (24 to 28 liters) of feed or grain, and 30 gallons (114 liters) of water—giant portions for giant horses.

There are three hitches of Anheuser-Busch Clydesdales. One hitch is based on the West Coast in Romoland, California; one is located on the East Coast in Merrimack, New Hampshire; and one is at the Anheuser-Busch corporate headquarters in St. Louis. Altogether, they log nearly 90,000 miles (145,000 kilometers) a year.

In order to move one hitch, three large tractor-trailers are required. Two of the tractor-trailers carry the horses. A team always travels with ten horses, eight for the hitch and two relief horses rotated into the hitch to allow other horses to rest. The third vehicle carries the red brewery wagon, harness, portable stalls, and all other equipment needed for the Clydesdales to make a personal appearance. Attending each appearance is a crew of six: two drivers and four grooms. As a symbol of days past, when the Dalmatian dog protected the horses and guarded the wagon, no hitch would be complete without a spotted canine on board.

Preparing the horses for an appearance is a five-hour operation. Although they are groomed daily, they get special attention before show time. Their legs are shampooed so that not a stain or speck of dirt will be found on their fluffy white "feathers." Their manes are rolled and braided with ribbon. Finally, bows are attached to their tails, which are kept short, or "docked," so that they do not become tangled in the harness and equipment.

Now the Clydesdales are ready to be put into harness. Each horse in the hitch is assigned a special position. The wheelers are the pair closest to the wagon. It is their job to both start and stop the wagon. The swing pair is next, and in front of them are the body horses. They are responsible for turning the wagon. The leaders are the front pair. They are the fastest horses on the team.

Beginning with the wheelers, each horse is equipped with a bridle and two bits, a back pad, and a 130-pound (60-kilogram) collar with the traditional Scotch spire decoration at the top. Each harness is fitted to the individual horse. Finally, the wagon is hitched to the horses, the two drivers take their places, and the Clydesdales are ready to roll.

For the drivers, controlling 12 tons of horses and wagon requires both strength and skill. The entire hitch, from the back of the wagon to the first horses, measures 75 feet (23 meters) in length. The reins in the driver's hands weigh 40 pounds (18 kilograms). All drivers are put through a training program before they can drive a hitch.

Left: Before an appearance, the "feathers" on a Clydesdale's legs are shampooed to a spotless white. Above: Decked out in custom-fitted harness, this Clydesdale is ready to take his place in the hitch.

The Clydesdales are a familiar sight all over the United States. They make an annual showing in the Orange Bowl Parade in Miami, Florida, and the Tournament of Roses Parade in Pasadena, California. They have appeared at world's fairs, state fairs, and racetracks. They also visit hospitals, orphanages, and retirement homes. A hitch horse usually spends about ten years in service. After that, he is retired either to one of the home bases or to one of three theme parks owned by Anheuser-Busch.

Although the term "horsepower" now indicates the power of an engine, the Clydesdale is a magnificent reminder of a time when the word meant exactly what it said. From plowing fields to pulling heavy wagons, these horses have served willingly. Their tradition will not die as long as the low rumble of wagon wheels, the slap of leather reins, and the jingling of brass harness continue to thrill onlookers.

Boomerang

SUCCESS IN FOURS

It is impossible to separate the Irish from their horses. They have depended on each other for their daily existence for generations. It is no surprise, then, that a country so rich in horse tradition would invent one of the most exciting equestrian sports—show jumping. It should also come as no surprise that an Irish horse and rider would redefine the terms of that sport.

Eddie Macken was a butcher's son, the youngest of five children. While his father had no objection to Eddie riding, he hoped that his son would follow a more traditional career than that of working with horses. But all Eddie wanted to do was ride the pony his father had bought him.

Macken received his early training from the village veterinarian, Brian Gormley. He would take Eddie and his pony out to the Irish countryside in a "pony and trap," a small one-horse carriage. There, they unhitched the pony, and Gormley gave the boy his first lessons on horseback.

Gormley soon recognized Macken's talent on a horse. As Macken's love of horses did not lessen, Gormley took him to Iris Kellet, a famous Irish rider, for more advanced training. It was at Kellet's barn in County Kildare that he first met Boomerang.

Boomerang's origins were as Irish as Macken's. His sire was the Thoroughbred stallion Battleburn. His mother, The Girl From Brown Mountain, was a cross between a Thoroughbred and an Irish draft horse. The mare was owned by a farmer, James Murphy of Grangemockler. Like many Irish farmers, Murphy had decided to breed his mare, figuring her foal might be worth something as a hunter someday.

Born in 1966, the bay colt grew to be 16 hands 2 inches tall, and was taught to work under saddle. As a four-year-old, he was used in the hunt. Watching the horse develop, Murphy suspected that the gelding he had named Battleboy might have talent as a show jumper. So Murphy took the horse to the Kellet's barn for training.

Eddie Macken was working for Kellet in the early 1970s when she paired them as a team. In later years Kellet would say that the horse who became Boomerang was as raw as the twenty-year-old Macken when they first met. Horse and rider did not take to each other at first, for as talented as Battleboy was, he proved very difficult in training. And in fact, the horse would change hands several times over the next few years before his partnership with Macken really began.

Macken rode him at the Dublin Spring Show the year after he arrived at Kellet's. There the horse was seen by the Irish trainer Tommy Brennan. Brennan immediately telephoned a friend, the well-known English trainer Ted Edgar, suggesting that the horse might be worth purchasing. Edgar flew to Ireland and bought the horse, and Battleboy was shipped to England.

Eddie Macken and Boomerang became one of the most famous teams in show jumping. Here they clear an obstacle at the 1979 European Championships.

Edgar's wife, Liz, now worked the horse. As difficult and ornery as Battleboy was, she did not allow him to frustrate her. She took time with the horse and proceeded with great patience. She also changed his name. At a local schooling show, she mentioned to some Australian friends that she did not like the name Battleboy. As they discussed this problem over coffee and a tin of Australian "Boomerang" biscuits, her friends pointed to the lid of the biscuit tin. "Why don't you call him Boomerang?" they suggested. It was the name he would make famous.

In less than two years, Liz Edgar took Boomerang from competing at the local level to international competition. It was at one of these shows that Leon Melchior, an amateur rider from Belgium, spotted the horse and bought him—for ten times the price the Edgars had paid for him. Melchior put Boomerang in training with world-class rider Johann Heins.

At Olympia, the big Christmas competition in London, Belgian François Mathy rode the horse. Again, Boomerang proved trying and inconsistent. The horse nearly always jumped clean—that is, he seldom knocked down fences. But he frequently stopped short just before an obstacle, refusing to jump it at all. His performance at Olympia was less than brilliant.

But Olympic show-jumping champion Paul Schockemohle was in the stands that day, and with him was Eddie Macken. Macken wanted to train with Schockemohle. The two had agreed to meet at the Olympia show to work out the details of their arrangement. Secretly, Schockemohle thought the big bay would be a good mount for Macken. He told Macken he was thinking of buying Boomerang. "You don't want that horse," said Macken. Nonetheless, Schockemohle bought the horse for his sponsor, the German industrialist Herbert Schnapka. Both Boomerang and Macken now moved to Muhlen, Germany, to train with Schockemohle.

Macken had arrived in Germany with only one horse. Then, in 1975, just before a big competition in Wiesbaden, that horse was not able to compete. "Look," Schockemohle said to Macken, "you ride Boomerang until you get a better horse." It was at the Wiesbaden show that the Macken-Boomerang partnership took flight.

The horses and riders from Schockemohle's barn were winning almost every class. Macken and Boomerang had placed in several classes themselves. Then Schockemohle fell from his horse and broke his collarbone. He suggested that Macken take his place and ride Boomerang in the Grand Prix competition, the most demanding class of the show.

Boomerang's performance was still uneven, so Macken had been experimenting with different bits. The horse hated every bit that was put in his mouth. As a last resort, on the morning of the Grand Prix, Macken asked his groom to dig a hackamore out of the tack trunk. "It's the only thing we haven't tried," he said. With no bit in his mouth, Boomerang sailed around the Grand Prix course—and won, defeating thirty other riders.

For the rest of 1975, Boomerang and Macken traveled throughout Europe, England, and Ireland, entering all the major jumping competitions. Time after time, they won. The horse that had been sold because of his inconsistency became the most consistent horse in world show jumping.

But while Boomerang's behavior in the show ring was faultless, his attitude in his stall left something to be desired. In November 1977, Macken and Boomerang were at a competition in Austria. Macken's groom was leaving, and he needed a replacement. By chance, Fiona Dowley, an Irish groom, happened to be at that show. Macken asked her if she could help him finish out the year. She agreed and took over the care of Macken's four competition horses, including Boomerang.

No one had warned Dowley that Boomerang had a way of "talking you out of his stall." When she went into the stall the first time, to hang up a water bucket, he flattened his ears and swung his back end toward his new groom. Dowley scrambled up the bars of the stall and climbed out. After that, she always made sure she had an escape route.

It took two months for Dowley to gain Boomerang's trust. But after that rude introduction, they became great friends. Dowley came to feel that Boomerang was her horse and, rather than just finishing out the year, she remained with Boomerang for the rest of his life.

Boomerang was particular about who handled him and for what purpose. He would allow only Dowley to take him from his stall and groom and saddle him. After he was tacked up, he preferred only Macken in the saddle.

At the end of the 1977 show season, Macken wanted to return home to Ireland. He had purchased a farm there, Rafeehan Stud. But how would this change affect his partnership with Boomerang? The horse was still owned by Herbert Schnapka.

Macken made arrangements with a sponsor, Carroll's Tobacco Company, to help him purchase Boomerang. But when he approached Schnapka with the plan, the owner rejected the idea. He felt that the partnership between horse and rider was exceptional. He gave Boomerang to Eddie Macken. So, for Christmas 1977, Macken and Boomerang returned home to Rafeehan Stud. Carroll's Tobacco Company still sponsored the horse, paying his showing expenses in the years to come. For this reason, Boomerang's name was changed again—to Carroll's Boomerang.

Over the next three years, Macken and Boomerang competed ten months out of every year. As they traveled from show to show, their reputation grew. The crowds cheered whenever Boomerang and Macken came into the show ring. The pair became national heroes.

Word got around that Boomerang's favorite treat was Polo Mints, a round flat candy. Boomerang fans sent boxes of the mints to their favorite horse. Mail arrived at Rafeehan Stud addressed simply, "Boomerang, Ireland." At Christmastime, Boomerang received his own cards.

Boomerang thrived on work. He set records that still stand. He also seemed to achieve his successes in groups of four. He had four clear rounds in his first year competing at the World Championships. He became the only horse to win both major classes of the challenging Wembley competition in England four times. He won the Victor Ludorum competition at the Horse of the Year Show in England four times. And for four years in a row, he competed as part of the Irish team at Ireland's big show, the Aga Khan, without knocking down a single fence.

In each of the few times he did come in second, it was a narrow miss. In 1978, Boomerang and Macken competed at the World Championships at Aachen, Germany. There were three days of competition. The first day was a speed class, the winner being whoever finished the course the fastest with the fewest faults. The second and third days of competition each consisted of two jumping classes. After these classes, the faults that each rider earned in each round of competition were added together. (In show jumping, horse and rider accumulate four faults if they knock down a fence, and time faults if they finish the course over the allowed time limit, ¼ fault for each second over.) The four top horses and riders—the ones with the fewest faults—then competed against each other for the world title.

Eddie Macken and Boomerang were in the top four. Their competition for the final jump-off was stiff: Gord Wiltfang of Germany, Michael Matz of the United States, and Boomerang's former rider, Johann Heins of Belgium. To make matters even more challenging, each of the riders had to ride the horses of the other three. Each rider was given exactly one minute to acquaint himself with the unfamiliar mount. Then the bell was rung, and horse and rider faced the toughest course in the world.

Fiona Dowley hoped that Boomerang's unwillingness to be ridden by anybody but Macken would guarantee the pair the World Championship. But at this stage of his career, Boomerang was fit and his timing was keen. He also loved to win. He cooperated beautifully with the other three riders.

Macken performed well on the horses belonging to Matz and Wiltfang. But on Heins's Dutch warmblood, he came in $\frac{2}{10}$ of a second over the time limit. He was penalized with $\frac{1}{4}$ time fault and lost the World Championship.

In the following year, the pair competed in the Netherlands. One of the jumps on the course was a water jump. In order to clear this type of jump without faults, the horse must land without any part of his hoof in the water. When Macken and Boomerang took the water jump, the judge signaled a fault. The crowd booed. To everyone else, it appeared that the pair had cleared the obstacle. But the judge's decision stood— and cost Macken and Boomerang the European championship.

Boomerang responded to this disappointment by living up to his name: He came back strong one week later, at the Hickstead Derby in Ireland.

It was a miserable day. A steady rain made the course slick and soupy. Boomerang hated mud, and the thirty-three other horses and riders preceding him were churning the course into a sea of brown muck. Boomerang was the last to compete. But the rain let up just as he entered the arena, and he won the Hickstead for an unprecedented fourth time in a row.

Again, Macken was presented with the gold Hickstead trophy. After each of the other three wins, he had to return the trophy to the

*Boomerang's talent and power were tested to the
limit over daunting obstacles like this huge spread
jump, at the 1978 World Championships.*

Derby officials. But with this victory, he could keep the trophy. Hickstead officials had to order a new trophy for future competitions—a bronze statuette of Eddie Macken and Boomerang coming down the famous Derby Bank at Hickstead.

In 1980, after he won the Braintree match at Essex in England, Boomerang returned to Rafeehan Stud. One day, while Macken's wife, Suzanne, was exercising him, he went lame. The X rays showed that a chip had broken from a bone in his right front foot.

While Boomerang's front feet had often given him trouble, he had so much "heart" that he did not let them interfere with his jumping career. This injury, however, he could not overcome. Macken retired him immediately. Hickstead gave Boomerang a retirement ceremony, presenting him with a blanket of roses. He then returned home to Rafeehan Stud to enjoy a quieter life.

Three years after his retirement, Boomerang developed an infection in his front hoof. The infection spread so rapidly that it was beyond treatment. Macken made the difficult decision to have the horse put to sleep. Boomerang was buried at Rafeehan Stud, in a grave surrounded by four evergreen trees.

Macken and Boomerang were great popular favorites, especially in Ireland. A crowd gathered to see the horse make his last public appearance there, in 1982.

Cass Olé

THE BLACK STALLION

The image of the Black Stallion has stirred the imagination of readers ever since Walter Farley created the fictitious desert horse in 1941. Generations of readers have been held spellbound by the adventures of the free-spirited Arabian horse and the boy who loves him. So far-reaching was the impression left by the Black that more than thirty years after the book was first published, Zoetrope Studios decided to make it into a movie.

But who would play the part of the Black? Obviously it would take a special animal to portray a horse that had lived so long in the hearts and minds of readers. For months the film's director, Carroll Ballard, looked at horses in the United States, Canada, and Europe. The quest ended in Texas with the discovery of the Arabian stallion Cass Olé.

When he was born at the Donoghue Farm on March 6, 1969, few would have guessed that Cass Olé was destined to be a movie star. In fact, he was rather odd-looking.

The Black Stallion *and* The Black Stallion Returns *tell the story of a beautiful Arabian horse, played on screen by Cass Olé.*

Arabian horses that eventually become black are not born that color. In fact, the foal coat is mouse-gray. Because black is a rare color in Arabians, it is not uncommon for a breeder to ponder the unusual-looking foal coat and wonder what color the animal would eventually become.

When Arabian breeding authority James Dean visited the Donoghue Farm, he and owner Gerald Donoghue puzzled over the colt's odd color. Because of the foal's mouse-colored coat, Dean called him Mickey Mouse. Later, as Mickey Mouse began to lose his baby fuzz, Donoghue noticed the dark color of the underlying coat.

While Mickey Mouse was fine for a nickname, the colt still needed a name that could be listed in the Arabian Horse Registry. Donoghue wanted to include the name Cass in the name to refer to the foal's sire, Al-Marah Cassanova. As his mother's name, La Bahia, was Spanish, they wanted something Spanish-sounding to honor her. "Let's call him Cass Olé," suggested Gerald Donoghue. "Then, when he enters the show ring, everyone can get up and shout, "Olé! Olé!"

Cass Olé didn't wait long to begin his show career. He took second in a class of yearling colts at his first show, in San Antonio. Then, at a show in Dallas, he took first place in the Most Classic class, in which the horses are judged on how well they measure up to true Arabian type. It was these classic Arabian looks that would later win him the movie role.

As a two-year-old, Cass was sent to trainer Walter Chapman to be put under saddle. It was there that he met Francesca Cuello, an eleven-year-old riding student. Under Chapman's watchful eye, Francesca and Cass began to work together. They did so well in their training sessions that Francesca's father offered to buy the horse from the Donoghues.

Donoghue wasn't at all certain about selling a stallion for a young-ster to ride. But Arabian stallions are known for their even temperaments. In fact, Arabian stallions are the only stallions that the American Horse Shows Association will allow junior riders (those under eighteen) to show. Cass Olé was such a gentleman that Donoghue eventually agreed and sold him to the Cuellos.

Francesca and Cass became a successful team. Over the course of their show career, they won 750 awards. Cass proved his versatility by winning in many different kinds of competition—Western pleasure, English pleasure, driving, native costume, and sidesaddle. Once, in a hotly contested sidesaddle class, Gerald Donoghue's prophecy was fulfilled. The competition was so close that the crowd stood and shouted "Olé! Olé!" to show the judges its preference.

In 1974 the American Horse Shows Association named Cass Horse of the Year for all breeds and also awarded him the King Saud Cup, a prize given to the Arabian horse who has earned the most points in all divisions. Cass won both prizes again the following year and was also named national champion in Arabian Western pleasure.

It was while Cass was showing at the Arabian Nationals in Kentucky in 1976 that he came to the attention of writer Walter Farley. Farley knew of the difficulty the production company was having in finding the right horse for the film version of his book. He was impressed by Cass Olé's performance and mentioned the horse to producer Francis Ford Coppola. Coppola, however, was not convinced that this was the horse they wanted, for Cass Olé was not completely black; he had four white socks and a star. But Farley insisted, and Cass Olé was moved to the Randall Ranch in California, where he began special training for the movie with Corky Randall.

Randall's father had developed his own methods of training horses to perform in films. The horse was taught to respond to different positions of a long whip held by the trainer off camera. Cass Olé proved to be a quick study. That was fortunate because Randall was given only three months to train him before Cass began working in front of the cameras.

But first, Cass Olé's white markings had to be dyed black. Two chestnut quarter horses had been chosen as his "stunt doubles," and they also needed to be dyed, to match Cass. Randall stocked up on packages of women's blue-black hair coloring and dyed all three horses. Dyeing a horse is a long process. It must be done right the first time because horsehair will not take the dye a second time. (Later, when "touch-ups" were needed on Cass's star and socks, Randall used black eyeliner.) With preparations completed, Cass was shipped to Canada to shoot his scenes.

At best, movie work is slow and painstaking. But Cass liked the work and liked the people. In fact, he took to the picture business so well that he didn't need to be led on a halter and lead rope from one camera setup to the next. He simply followed trainer Corky Randall. "You're not going to get many horses like Cass," said Randall.

Still, there are times on a movie set that will fray the best of temperaments. On days when Cass decided that he'd had enough, he would simply leave the set and go stand by the horse van.

Since movies are filmed out of sequence, scenes that occur in the middle and at the end of the picture were shot first. Cass did about 80 percent of the work in the film. But when the action was considered too dangerous for the "star," one of his stunt doubles was used.

After these scenes were "in the can," Cass and his doubles were loaded onto an airplane and flown to Italy. The producers had chosen the island of Sardinia off the coast of Italy to represent the desert island off the coast of North Africa where Alec Ramsey and the Black are shipwrecked at the beginning of the book.

In several scenes, the Black had to seem uncontrollable, rearing and
striking at enemies. In fact, Cass was taught to make these moves in
response to a trainer's signals, and they were well rehearsed.

These were demanding sequences for Cass Olé as he worked on camera either alone or only with Kelly Reno, who played Alec. In all of these scenes, Cass was "at liberty," meaning he was not contained or restrained in any way. He had to watch and obey his trainer, who, off camera, guided the horse in all his movements.

To make sure that each scene was right, director Carroll Ballard shot the scenes on the island over and over again. Filming on Sardinia began in the late summer, and the weather turned rainy and cold with the approach of fall. Still, Cass took it all in stride and managed to have a little fun as well.

One evening, Cass, Kelly Reno, and the small crew were walking back from the set. That day's work had included some of the sequences in which Alec rides the Black for the first time. Cass was wet from being in and out of the water. A horse likes nothing so much as a good roll when he is wet, and the sand on the beach looked inviting. Cass began to paw. Quickly, director of photography Caleb Deschanel shouldered his camera, and the resulting footage of Cass Olé and Kelly Reno rolling in the sand was used at the end of the film while the credits rolled.

For the underwater sequence in which the Black Stallion swims to the rescue boat, Cass once again was doubled, this time by two Camargue ponies. Director Ballard wanted a specific "look" to the underwater movement of the horse. So Corky Randall brought in the ponies from the Camargue region of southern France. These two "white horses of the sea" were dyed black, and the high-stepping action for which the breed is noted was photographed underwater.

At last, filming was completed, and Cass Olé returned home to Texas. What awaited him was the biggest challenge of his life.

Shortly after Cass had left for California, Francesca was in a bad accident. Now seventeen, she was hauling one of the family's horses to the trainer's barn. The truck she was driving flipped three times, and she was thrown from the vehicle. She was unconscious for three weeks.

While she lay in a coma, Francesca's mother and father, both doctors, talked to her, just as if she were awake. When she finally did wake up, her parents encouraged her through the long healing process by telling her that Cass had returned and was waiting for her to ride him.

When Francesca was able to leave the hospital, Cass helped her with her physical therapy. Wearing a helmet, Francesca was lifted onto Cass Olé's back. At first, Cass moved slowly. As Francesca rode him at the walk, her weak muscles began to gain strength. Much later, she was able to ride and show Cass again.

Released in 1979, the film *The Black Stallion* was an immediate success. Cass Olé became an instant celebrity and Zoetrope made plans to produce a sequel, *The Black Stallion Returns*, which was released four years later. To promote the films, Cass made personal appearances all over the country. He had become so famous that he was invited to appear in President Ronald Reagan's first inaugural parade, in January 1981. Thanks to Cass, Francesca was well enough to ride him in that parade.

Both before and after his movie career, Cass Olé was used as a breeding stallion. He produced a total of 120 registered purebred Arabian foals, 50 of which were black. But far more important than color were the qualities of temperament, athletic ability, and versatility that Cass passed on to his offspring.

Cass Olé died on July 22, 1993. But for millions, he will live forever on film as the Black Stallion.

GLOSSARY

bank—A show jumping obstacle that includes an earthen mound; the horse jumps up on and down off the bank.

bit—A device placed in a horse's mouth to help control direction, pace, and head position; made of metal or rubber, it is attached to the bridle and reins.

bridle—A piece of equipment that buckles around the horse's head and to which reins are attached.

broodmare—A mare used for breeding.

canter—A slow, controlled gallop, the canter is a three-beat gait. If the horse is cantering to the right, its feet strike the ground in this order: left hind, right hind and left fore together, and right fore.

clear round—In show jumping, a round without faults.

collar—A piece of harness that fits over the horse's shoulders and takes the strain of pulling a load.

colt—A male horse less than four years old.

course—In show jumping, a group of obstacles to be jumped in a set order.

cross—To breed two different types (such as the Arab and the English horse).

dam—The mother of a horse.

draft horse—A horse bred to pull heavy loads.

dressage—A systematic method of training horses to perform movements in a relaxed, balanced, supple, and obedient way.

faults—In show jumping, points used to record knockdowns, refusals, and other errors.

filly—A female horse less than four years old.

foal—A horse less than a year old.

gait—The horse's way of going. There are three natural gaits: walk, trot, and canter (or gallop).

gallop—The fastest natural gait (see canter).

gelding—A castrated male horse.

girth—A strap that passes under the horse's belly to hold the saddle in place.

hackamore—A bitless bridle.

hand—A unit used in measuring a horse's height. One hand equals 4 inches (about 10 centimeters); a horse that stands 16 hands measures 64 inches (163 centimeters) from the ground to the highest point of the withers.

hitch—To hook up (a horse or team of horses) to a wagon.

hunter—A horse used in hunting, usually to follow hounds in foxhunting.

jump-off—In show jumping, a round held to decide the winner from competitors who have tied for first place in the previous round.

length—The length of a horse's head and body, a distance by which a horse may be said to have won a race.

lunge line—A flat piece of webbing, usually 25 to 30 feet (8 to 9 meters) long, used to train or exercise horses from the ground by working them in a circle.

mare—A female horse aged four years or older.

mustang—A wild horse of the American West.

neck—The length of a horse's head and neck, a distance by which a horse may be said to have won a race.

reins—Narrow straps attached to the bit or bridle and used by a rider or driver to guide a horse and control its pace.

sire—The father of a horse.

stallion—A male horse aged four years or older.

stud—A stallion used for breeding.

tack—Stable gear, especially equipment such as saddles and bridles used in riding.

Thoroughbred—A breed developed for racing; founded by crossing Arabian stallions on English mares.

trot—A two-beat gait in which the horse's feet strike the ground in diagonal pairs; that is, right hind and left fore together, and then left hind and right fore.

walk—A four-beat gait in which the feet strike left hind, left front, right hind, right front. At least two feet are on the ground at all times.

warmblood—Any of several European breeds originated by breeding Thoroughbred, Arabian, and similar horses with heavier breeds. Warmbloods are often used in dressage and show jumping.

water jump—A show jumping obstacle that includes a wide sunken trough filled with water.

weanling—A foal that no longer needs its dam's milk. Foals are usually separated from their dams when they are four to six months old.

weight—In racing, the amount of weight a horse is required to carry. If the rider and saddle do not weigh enough, lead blocks are inserted in a special saddle cloth.

withers—The point where a horse's neck meets its back.

yearling—A horse in its second year of life.

FURTHER READING

Ancona, George. *Man and Mustang*. New York: Macmillan, 1992.

Bongianni, Maurizo. *Simon and Schuster's Guide to Horses and Ponies of the World*. New York: Simon and Schuster/Fireside Books, 1987.

Coleman, Alix, and Steven D. Price. *All the King's Horses: The Story of the Budweiser Clydesdales*. New York: Viking Press, 1983.

Edwards, Elwyn Hartley. *The Ultimate Horse Book*. New York: Dorling Kindersley, 1991.

Farley, Walter. *The Black Stallion*. New York: Random House, 1977.

MacGregor, Morris. *The World's Show Jumpers*. South Brunswick: Barnes, 1967.

Rodenas, Paula. *The Random House Book of Horses & Horsemanship*. New York: Random House, 1991.

Sayer, Angela. *The Young Rider's Handbook*. New York: Arco Publishing, Inc., 1984.

Wear, Terri. *Horse Stories*. Metuchen: Scarecrow, 1987.

INDEX

ABOUT THE AUTHOR

Laurel van der Linde is a breeder and
trainer of Arabian horses as well as a writer.

Her previous books for young readers include
The Pony Express and *The White Stallions:
The Story of the Dancing Horses of Lippiza*,
as well as *The Devil in Salem Village:
The Story of the Salem Witchcraft Trials*
in the Spotlight on American History series
from The Millbrook Press.

She lives in Castaic, California.